DISCARD

Countries Around the World

Latvia

Claire Throp

SOUTH HUNTINGTON
PUBLIC LIBRARY
145 PIDGEON HILL RD
HUNT. STA., NY 11746

Heinemann Library
Chicago, Illinois

www.heinemannraintree.com

Visit our website to find out more information about Heinemann-Raintree books.

To order:

☎ Phone 888-454-2279

🖥 Visit www.heinemannraintree.com to browse our catalog and order online.

© 2012 Heinemann Library
an imprint of Capstone Global Library, LLC
Chicago, Illinois

All rights reserved. No part of this publication may be reproduced or transmitted in any form or by any means, electronic or mechanical, including photocopying, recording, taping, or any information storage and retrieval system, without permission in writing from the publisher.

Edited by Kate de Villiers and Vaarunika Dharmapala
Designed by Joanna Hinton-Malivoire
Original illustrations © Capstone Global Library Ltd 2011
Illustrated by Oxford Designers & Illustrators
Picture research by Ruth Blair
Originated by Capstone Global Library Ltd
Printed and bound in China by CTPS

15 14 13 12 11
10 9 8 7 6 5 4 3 2 1

Library of Congress Cataloging-in-Publication Data
Throp, Claire.
  Latvia / Claire Throp.
     p. cm.—(Countries around the world)
  Including bibliographical references and index.
  ISBN 978-1-4329-5211-2 (hardcover)—ISBN 978-1-4329-5236-5 (pbk.) 1. Latvia—Juvenile literature. I. Title.
  DK504.23.T4 2012
  947.96—dc22   2010039277

Acknowledgments
We would like to thank the following for permission to reproduce photographs: p. **27** Alamy (© vario images GmbH & Co.KG); Getty Images p. **10** (David Rubinger/Time Life Pictures), p. **33** (Walter Iooss Jr. /Sports Illustrated); iStockphoto p. **9** (© Ints Vikmanis), p. **18** (© Indars Grasbergs), p. **19** (© Ian Sargent), p. **25** (© Jurijs Korjakins), p. **34** (© Paul Pegler); Photolibrary p. **35**; Shutterstock p. **5** (© Richards), p. **7** (© Nikonaft), p. **8** (© Tupungato), p. **13** (© Andrejs Jegorovs), pp. **14, 15** (© krosbona), p. **16** (© Renars Jurkovskis), p. **17** (© syaochka), p. **21** (© Ainars Aunins), p. **23** (© Andrejs Jegorovs), p. **25** (© Julien), p. **29** (© Nikonaft), p. **31** (© Ints Vikmanis), p. **37** (© Ludmila Pankova), p. **39** (© Nikonaft), p. **46** (© pdesign).

Cover photograph of Riga reproduced with permission of Getty Images (© Garron Nicholls/Flickr).

We would like to thank Daniel Block for his invaluable help in the preparation of this book.

Every effort has been made to contact copyright holders of material reproduced in this book. Any omissions will be rectified in subsequent printings if notice is given to the publisher.

Disclaimer
All the Internet addresses (URLs) given in this book were valid at the time of going to press. However, due to the dynamic nature of the Internet, some addresses may have changed, or sites may have changed or ceased to exist since publication. While the author and publisher regret any inconvenience this may cause readers, no responsibility for any such changes can be accepted by either the author or the publisher.

Contents

Some words in the book are in bold, **like this**. You can find out what they mean by looking in the glossary.

Introducing Latvia

What do you know about Latvia? You may have heard that Latvians love to sing. Their folk songs and song festivals are famous. The beauty of Riga, its capital city, is well known. Latvia also has many forests and deserted beaches.

Where is Latvia?

Latvia is officially known as the **Republic** of Latvia. The country is small—about the size of West Virginia. There are just under 2.3 million people in Latvia. It is one of the few countries to have a smaller population today than it did 20 years ago. This is partly due to Russians returning to Russia since Latvia's **independence**. About two-thirds of Latvians live in cities and towns.

Latvia has been described as sitting at the crossroads of northern and eastern Europe. It is one of the three Baltic States and is situated between Estonia and Lithuania.

Russian connection

Latvia has a history of invasion from other countries that wanted to use its important **trade** routes. For most of the 20th century, Latvia was under the control of Russia. This has resulted in a strong Russian influence today. It is thought that about 29 percent of the population is Russian. All three Baltic States have gained their independence since 1991.

Jelgava Palace is on the Lielupe River. It was built in 1738 for Count Ernst, one of the rulers of the area.

History: A Fight for Independence

There is evidence that people lived in the area that is now Latvia as early as 3000 BCE. However, the **tribes** that later became known as Latvians and Lithuanians didn't arrive until about 2000 BCE. Little is known about them. They settled along the coast and probably survived by fishing and hunting animals in the forests. Around 100 CE tribes began to **trade** valuable **amber** with the Romans.

German control

In the 1200s, German knights called the Livonian Brothers of the Sword invaded Latvia. The knights were sent by the Pope, the head of the Catholic Church, to bring Christianity to the Baltic tribes. At that time the tribes were **pagan**, a pre-Christian religion.

For hundreds of years, the Germans remained **dominant**. They considered themselves to be more important than the tribes-people. Non-Germans were not allowed to own property or be involved in government and were often treated as little more than slaves. Latvia became mainly Lutheran (**Protestant**) in the 1500s, as the German-speaking population took up the religion.

Foreign rule

From the mid-1550s to the early 1700s, Latvia was invaded a number of times. Poland and Lithuania took over much of what is now Latvia during the Livonian War (1558–1583). In the Polish-Swedish War, Sweden took control of Riga and the surrounding area in 1621. After the Northern War (1700–1721), Russia took over the land that Sweden had previously controlled.

The ruins of this ancient castle can be found in the town of Cēsis.

One nation

The 1800s saw Latvians gaining a sense of **national identity**. With the many changes of foreign rulers in previous years, this feeling of unity had not been possible. Russian rule had gradually provided Latvians with more freedom. Latvians were now allowed to go to universities and write about their own country in their own language. The first Latvian newspaper was published in 1822.

The "Latvian Awakening" movement

From 1873, many Latvians rose up against the dominant Germans and Russians. This came to be known as the "Latvian Awakening" movement. As a result of this movement, the first Latvian political party was created in 1904. The next year saw a **revolution**. There were widespread strikes and protests, and revolutionary Latvians set fire to German and Russian houses. Many of them were killed, and many others were sent into **exile**.

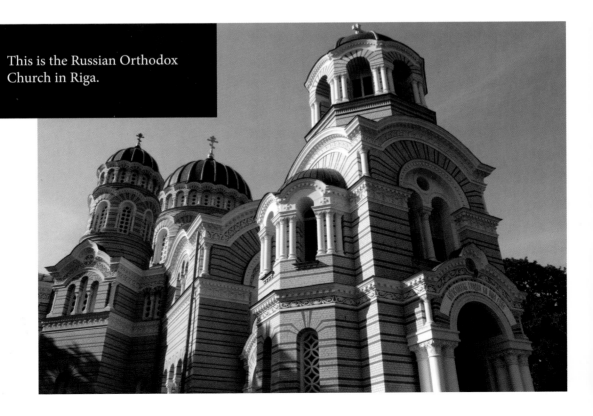

This is the Russian Orthodox Church in Riga.

War

During World War I (1914–1918), Latvia was invaded by Germany. By the end of the war, the country was divided between Germany and Russia. After Germany's defeat, Latvians saw the chance to gain **independence** in the "Liberation War." They declared independence for Latvia in 1918 along with the other Baltic States. Independence was recognized by Russia in 1920, and Latvia finally had the freedom it had wanted for so long.

The Freedom Monument was built in 1935 to celebrate Latvian independence.

JAÑIS RAINIS (1865–1929)

Poet and **playwright** Jānis Rainis was important in the fight for independence in the early 1900s. He wrote a play called *I Played and Danced* to encourage people to fight against foreign rule in Latvia.

World War II (1939–1945)

Unfortunately, Latvia's hard-won independence did not last long. World War II saw invasions first from Russia, then from Germany. Between 1940 and 1941, the Russians arrested thousands of Latvians and **deported** them to a distant country called Siberia. In 1941, the German army took control of Latvia. About 70,000 Latvian Jews and other **minorities** were killed. The population in Latvia was reduced to only 65 percent of its level in 1939. When Germany was defeated at the end of the war, Latvia was handed back to the Russians.

Regaining independence

After the war, many Russians moved to Latvia. School children were taught in Russian and Latvian. The Russians forced people to give up their privately owned land so that everyone could benefit from it.

The Popular Front of Latvia was set up in 1988. The group fought for freedom from Russian rule through protests and demonstrations.

The Baltic States are made up of Latvia, Estonia, and Lithuania.

These Latvians are protesting against Russian rule in 1990.

Freedom at last!

After Russian soldiers killed five demonstrators in January 1991, 74 percent of Latvians voted for independence. In 1991, Latvia's freedom was recognized around the world. The country joined the United Nations (**UN**) in 1991, and the North Atlantic Treaty Organization (**NATO**) and the European Union (**EU**) in 2004.

Financial crisis

The global financial crisis of 2008 affected Latvia badly. The country had to ask for help from the EU. Demonstrations against the government took place as financial cuts were put in place to try to rescue the country's **economy**. By 2010 the country's economy had improved, but the crisis was not over.

Regions and Resources: Forests, Lakes, and Rivers

Latvia's neighboring countries include the other Baltic States, Lithuania and Estonia, as well as Belarus and Russia. The coastline stretches 308 miles (497 kilometers) along the Baltic Sea and the Gulf of Riga.

The country is mainly flat, with a few rolling hills. The highest point, Gaizinkalns, is only 1,023 feet (312 meters) above sea level (see map below). Over 40 percent of the country is covered in forests, and there are many lakes and rivers.

Regions

There are five regions in Latvia: Kurzeme, Latgale, Zemgale, Vidzeme (which means "the middle of the country"), and the city of Riga. These regions are loosely based on areas where different **tribes** lived many years before.

This map shows the land height above sea level of Latvia and its neighbors.

In the west of Latvia is Kurzeme, an area made up of mostly farmland and a large section of Latvia's coastline. Zemgale is one of the wealthier areas in the middle of the country. Latgale in the south is the poorest area, partly because it is **rural** and there are few jobs available. However, it has some of the most beautiful scenery in the country. Gauja National Park, the largest national park in the country, is located within the Vidzeme region.

Climate

Latvia generally has short, warm summers and cold winters with a lot of snow. In coastal areas, the summer is often cooler and the winter warmer, making it milder than other countries in northern Europe.

While Latvia still gets plenty of snow in the winter months, some areas, such as western Kurzeme, have had less snow in recent years.

Lakes

There are 2,256 lakes in Latvia, covering more than 621 square miles (1,000 square kilometers). Nearly half of these lakes are in the eastern region of Latgale, which is known as "Land of Blue Lakes." Lake Lubāns is the largest lake, while the deepest is Dridzis. Velnezers Lake is also known as "The Devil's Lake." This is because the water seems to change color depending on the weather: green when it is sunny, and black when the weather is bad.

Daily life

Many of the lakes in the Latgale region are difficult for tour buses to reach because the roads are little more than dirt tracks. This means that Latvians are able to visit without running into many tourists. During the summer, families often go to the lakes to camp or stay in log cabins and take part in outdoor activities, such as mountain biking and rowing.

Latvia's most famous waterfall is the Ventas Rumba on the Venta River. In summer people go there to swim and stand on the stones in the middle of the waterfall.

The Gauja River is the longest in Latvia.

Rivers

The Daugava River begins in Russia and stretches for 634 miles (1,020 kilometers). Riga is one of the many towns and cities along its shores. There are also several **hydroelectric** power plants along the length of the river. The Lielupe River flows through the Zemgale region and eventually joins the Gulf of Riga. Lielupe means "big river," but it is actually only 74 miles (119 kilometers) long. The Gauja River is 280 miles (452 kilometers) long and flows through the Gauja National Park.

The coast

Latvia has just under 310 miles (500 kilometers) of coastline with many sandy beaches. In the Vidzeme region, the coastline includes spectacular sights, such as the Red Cliffs and fishing ports.

Resources

Forests, peat, limestone, and **amber** are among the natural resources of Latvia. Timber and amber are important **exports**, as are foods, such as fish and honey.

Amber

Amber was once used by local Latvian tribes to **trade** with the Romans. It was valued as much as gold in some areas of Europe. Latvians sometimes call the Baltic Sea the "Amber Sea" because this is where the amber comes from. It began as a sticky substance called resin that came out of pine trees. It was then fossilized over millions of years at the bottom of the Baltic Sea. Sometimes pieces of amber are found on the beach.

Trade

Latvia trades mainly with other Baltic States, Russia, and the United Kingdom. Oil has been found in the Kurzeme region, and Latvia has several hydroelectric power plants that provide energy. However, the country mainly relies on **imported** energy. Latvia also imports machinery and some foods.

Jobs

Farmland covers 39 percent of Latvia. Many people work in agricultural jobs, but the industry is in decline. The pharmaceutical (medicines) industry and new technology are recent growth areas. However, the biggest increase in jobs in recent years is in tourism.

Tourism is very important to Latvia's **economy**, particularly in the capital city of Riga. In 2006, over five million tourists from around the world were encouraged to visit Riga by offers of cheap flights to the city. Coastal resorts, such as Jūrmala, are also becoming popular tourist destinations.

Farming is an important part of Latvian life.

Wildlife: A Nature Paradise

Latvia is on the north-south **migration** route of many birds. Latvians are enthusiastic birdwatchers, and some people even set up posts for storks to nest on when they arrive in the spring. Many of the boggy **wetland** areas along the coast are protected so that there is plenty of food for birds.

White storks are thought to be lucky and bring protection from fire and lightning.

Latvia has a large beaver population and more wolves than the whole of the rest of northern Europe. Many animals that are rare elsewhere in Europe are common in Latvia, such as the European wolf and Eurasian otter.

Plants and trees

About 30 different types of orchid grow in Latvia, including a rare orchid called the lady's slipper. Ferns are among the most common plants in Latvia. Oak and linden trees can be found all over the country.

The Latvian Red Book

In 1977, the Latvian Red Book was created. It is a list of the **endangered** animals and plants in the country. Endangered animals in Latvia include ermine and martens. Ermine are similar to weasels, and martens are also small mammals. Violets and some types of orchids are among the rare plants.

Eurasian beavers are very common in Latvia.

Protected areas

Latvia has 684 specially protected nature areas. These include four national parks, one biosphere reserve, and 42 nature parks. Latvia also has over 900 micro-reserves. These are smaller areas that have been specially selected for the protection of rare species and their habitats.

Nature reserves

There are 259 nature reserves in Latvia. Lake Pape is a nature reserve in western Latvia. It is part of a project to bring back wild horses to Latvia. The horses died out in the 1700s. However, in 1999 Latvia **imported** 18 wild horses from Poland, and now there are more than 50.

The Teiči and Pelecares bogs are 10,000 years old. The area is protected, and no one can enter without a guide. Rare and endangered birds, such as cliff eagles and gray herons, stop there on their migrations.

National parks

The Gauja National Park includes the Gauja River and three towns: Sigulda, Cesis, and Ligatne. Along the banks of the Gauja River are cliffs, streams, and many caves. Gutmana Cave is in Sigulda and is 30 feet (9 meters) high and 59 feet (18 meters) deep. Many people like to go canoeing or hiking in the park.

The Kemeri National Park includes the wetland area, the Great Kemeri Bog. Among the ponds and moss are sundews, which are plants that trap insects and eat them. There are also huge numbers of birds feeding and nesting in the park, including black storks, woodpeckers, and eagles.

Ancient forests, swamps, and lakes can be found in Kemeri National Park. Many people like to follow the nature trails or visit bird-watching towers in the park.

This long line of semitrailers gives you an idea of just how many trees are being cut down in Latvia.

Environmental issues

One of the results of Russian rule was **pollution** of the air and rivers. Many factories were built that produced a lot of pollution. Old factory buildings and chimneys still spoil the landscape around many towns. However, since **independence** Latvia has worked hard to reduce pollution levels by about 46 percent. This has been helped by the shift toward services and tourism as main parts of the **economy**.

Deforestation

Another major issue for Latvia is the cutting down of large areas of trees, known as deforestation. The country's biggest **export** is timber. Forests currently cover about 44 percent of the land, but this percentage is decreasing. There are fears that forests are being cleared too quickly, giving them very little chance to recover. Older trees are being cut down, but they are not being replaced with enough new trees.

Recycling

Many people in Latvia still do not separate their trash into items that can be recycled and those that cannot. Organizations such as the Environmental Protection Club are concerned with protecting nature in Latvia and educating people about recycling. The club has about 3,400 members.

YOUNG PEOPLE

Garbage dumping is a problem in Latvia. "Project Footprints" encourages young people and their families to help clean up areas of Latvia. Projects have included clearing beaches of litter and preparing areas to be made into playgrounds for children. They even have trash-collecting competitions! Many children and schools get involved, as well as famous Latvians.

Infrastructure: Government and Education

Latvia has a parliamentary **democracy**. This means that Latvian **citizens** over 18 years old can vote for the people they want to represent them in parliament. Parliament—called the Saeima—has 100 members and is **elected** every four years. Presidential elections are also held every four years. The president is the **head of state** and is responsible for choosing the prime minister. The prime minister is the head of the government. He or she is responsible for the everyday running of the country.

Latvia is split up into 26 locally governed districts.

Economy

After **independence**, the growth rate of Latvia's **economy** was one of the highest in Europe. (It grew by 50 percent between 2004 and 2007.) However, the global financial crisis that began in 2008 hit Latvia hard. The country needed to ask for money loans from the **EU** and other organizations to help stabilize the economy.

The Latvian currency is the *lats*. There are 100 *santīmi* to one *lats*. The currency was introduced in 1993, after independence from Russia.

Media and technology

There are newspapers and television channels available in both Latvian and Russian. The most popular Latvian newspaper is *Diena,* with a readership of about 55,000.

Internet usage in Latvia is the lowest in the EU but, as of 2009, about 60 percent of people used the Internet at least once a week. There are now many Internet cafés in the cities, particularly in Riga. Use of cell phones is becoming more common than landlines.

Health care

Latvia has some free health care, which is controlled by local government and available to all citizens. The World Health Organization has ranked Latvia 105th in the world for their health care system.

A school day

Children in Latvia have to go to school between the ages of 7 and 16. They have two terms in a year, which means a long summer vacation. Do you think your summer vacation is long? Latvians get three months off! The school day usually lasts from 8:30 a.m. until 3:00 p.m., Monday through Friday.

There is a Latvian law that states there should be no more than 30 children in a class. Sometimes, particularly in **rural** areas, there can be as few as eight children in a class.

High school

Most children in Latvia go to high school, but some go to vocational school. Vocational schools allow students to train for a particular job, although they still have to study certain subjects, such as math and Latvian. There are also schools that focus on either sciences or humanities (subjects such as history and geography). Nearly every city has a music school and an art school. These are very popular and often provide accommodation for students who don't live in the city.

These Latvian children are learning Russian.

Language issues

In 1998, a law was passed that said Latvian was the only language to be used in high schools. Thousands protested against this law, and it was amended to allow 40 percent of lessons to be taught in a foreign language, such as Russian. Fewer pupils are now taught in Russian.

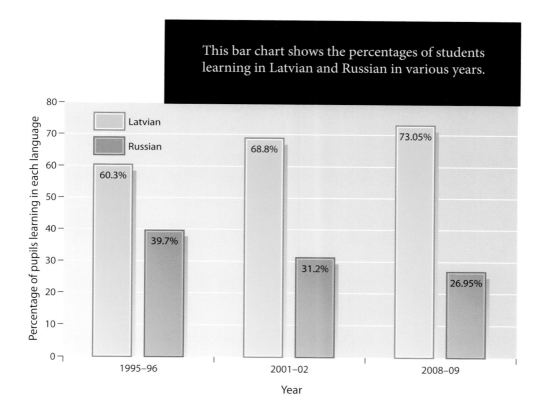

This bar chart shows the percentages of students learning in Latvian and Russian in various years.

YOUNG PEOPLE

Latvian teenagers usually dress in jeans and T-shirts and like to spend time with their friends in a local Internet café or at movie theaters. They go skateboarding and play sports, such as soccer in summer, and ski or play ice hockey in the winter.

Culture: Singing, Sports, and Art Nouveau

Riga is Latvia's capital city. The Old Town section of the city is famous for its beautiful Art Nouveau buildings. Art Nouveau is an early 20th-century art movement. It created decoration with flowing lines based on plants, shells, and animals. In 1997, Riga's Old Town was listed as a **UNESCO World Heritage site**. The World Heritage organization tries to protect areas of the world that are of outstanding natural and **cultural** importance.

European Capital of Culture 2014

Riga has been chosen as one of the European Capitals of **Culture** for 2014. Every year since 1985, a city has been named a European Capital of Culture. It was originally planned as a way to bring members of the **EU** together, focusing on culture rather than politics. From 2011, two cities will be given the title each year. Winning the title has usually resulted in increased tourism, as people are encouraged to visit the city to experience its unique culture.

MARK ROTHKO (1903–1970)

Artist Mark Rothko was born in what is now Daugavpils in Latvia. His family moved to the United States when he was 10 years old. His best-known paintings are those with several brightly colored rectangles on top of each other. He never returned to Latvia and died in 1970.

Literature

Latvia's most famous writers include Jānis Rainis, who wrote poems and plays in the late 1800s, and Karlis Skalbe, who is known for writing dark fairy tales for adults. Andrējs Pumpurs wrote down Latvia's folk stories, which until then were usually passed on by word of mouth.

This is one of the Art Nouveau buildings in Riga's Old Town, dating from 1905.

Singing

The first Song and Dance Festival took place in Latvia in 1873. Every four or five years choirs from all over the country wear national dress and perform together on outdoor stages. More than 30,000 people get involved.

Singing and dancing are closely connected to the Latvians' sense of **national identity**. There are believed to be over 1.2 million Latvian folk songs. A common saying claims that there is "one for every Latvian"! They are often sung at family celebrations such as birthdays and weddings.

This parade through Riga is part of the Latvian Youth Song and Dance Festival in 2010.

Daily life

Most countries in Europe think of the Eurovision Song Contest as just a bit of fun. Latvians take it very seriously! They won in 2002 with "I Wanna" sung by Marija Naumova, which led to Latvians celebrating in the streets.

Sports

Ice hockey is by far the most popular sport in Latvia. There are more than 3,000 players. The Latvian Hockey Federation was set up after Latvia achieved **independence**. By 1997, they had already reached the top ten of countries in the world playing the sport. Of huge excitement to Latvians was the staging of the 2006 World Ice Hockey Championships in Riga.

Tennis, basketball, and volleyball are also popular, but soccer is a growing sport, particularly after the national team did so well to qualify in the European Championships in 2004. Winter sports include skiing and bobsledding in the Gauja valley.

ULJANA SEMJONOVA (BORN 1952)

Uljana Semjonova is a former basketball player who was born in a village called Medumi in the Daugavpils district. She was one of the best women basketball players of the 1970s and 80s. It helped that she is about 6 foot 10 inches (2.12 meters) tall! She won two Olympic gold medals with the Russian basketball team in 1976 and 1980.

Traditional foods

Meat, rye bread, potatoes, and dairy products make up many Latvian dishes. Fish is also popular near the coast, and freshwater fish from rivers is seen as a luxury. Pork chops are a favorite meal. Beekeeping is common in Latvia, and honey is used to sweeten many foods.

Mealtime

Breakfast for Latvians nearly always includes a glass of milk. Many people eat cereal, eggs, or a sandwich. Traditionally, lunch is the main meal of the day, and it is usually a hot meal with several courses. The evening meal is usually smaller—sometimes just a sandwich. Families generally like to eat together, and second helpings are common!

A popular pastime in Latvia is picking mushrooms or berries in the forests so the ingredients are as fresh as possible for cooking. Sometimes people organize competitions to see who can pick the most!

Debessmanna recipe

Debessmanna is a whipped berry (cranberry or blueberry) dessert with milk. Ask an adult to help you make it.

Ingredients:
- ¾ cup cranberries (or blueberries)
- 2 cups water
- ½ cup sugar
- 5 tablespoons semolina

What to do:

1. Rinse and crush the cranberries. Squeeze out the juice.
2. Place the berries in a saucepan and cover with water. Leave to boil for five minutes and then strain. Add the sugar.
3. Gradually add the semolina, stirring all the time. Heat until the semolina thickens, and then add the cranberry juice.
4. Pour the mixture into a bowl and allow to cool. Use a whisk to whip the mixture until it has doubled or tripled in size.
5. Serve with cold milk.

Latvia Today

The relationship between Latvians and Russians living in Latvia today is a difficult one. After **independence**, a law was passed to say only people who had been living in Latvia before World War II—and their **descendants**— could be **citizens**. Everyone else would have to pass Latvian language and history tests before being granted citizenship.

Many Russians living in Latvia feel they are being treated badly. They cannot vote because only Latvian citizens are allowed to vote in elections. Membership in the **EU** has made the situation worse, as the Russians who have not passed or refuse to take the citizenship tests are unable to move and work within the EU. What do you think? Think about the history of Latvia. Are the Latvians right to treat the Russians in this way?

Latvian pride

National identity is very important to Latvians. They are very proud of their country, its **culture**, and its unspoiled natural beauty. Joining the EU in 2004 is often seen as a turning point. It has helped Latvia to develop relationships with other European countries and has increased their standing in the rest of the world. More and more people from around the world are choosing to visit Latvia.

YOUNG PEOPLE

Many families have moved from Riga to Jūrmala on the coast. Jūrmala is close to the capital city and also has a lot of water sports activities for adults and children. The Līvu Akvapark is the largest water theme park in northern Europe. It is a huge building with waterslides, whirlpools, and even its own river!

This is one of Jūrmala's peaceful sandy beaches.

Fact File

Official name:	**Republic** of Latvia
Government:	parliamentary **democracy**
Capital:	Riga
Bordering countries:	Estonia, Russia, Belarus, and Lithuania
Language:	Latvian with some Russian and Lithuanian
Population:	2,217,969
Birth rate:	9.9 births per 1,000 people
Life expectancy (total):	72.42
Life expectancy (men):	67.27
Life expectancy (women):	77.6
Religions (%):	Lutheran (19.6%)
	Orthodox (15.3%)
	other Christian (1%)
	other (0.4%)
Ethnic groups (%):	Latvian (58%)
	Russian (29%)
	Belarusian (3.6%)
	Ukrainian (2.5%)
	Polish (2.4%)
	Lithuanian (1.3%)
	other (3.2%)

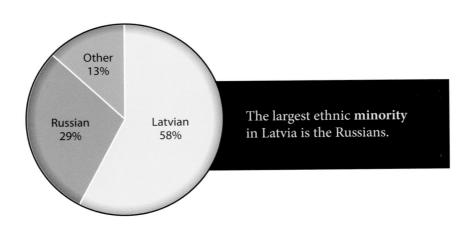

Other 13%

Russian 29%

Latvian 58%

The largest ethnic **minority** in Latvia is the Russians.

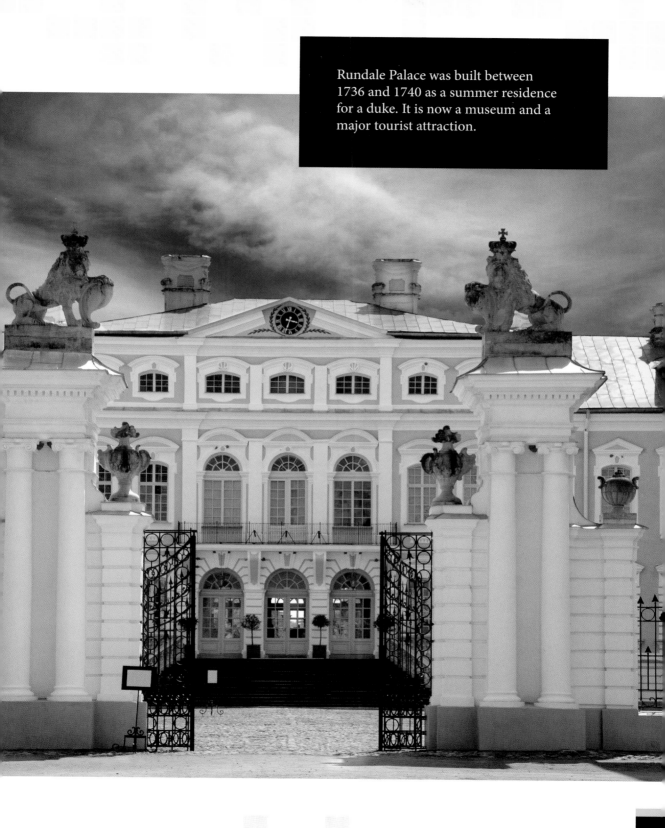

Rundale Palace was built between 1736 and 1740 as a summer residence for a duke. It is now a museum and a major tourist attraction.

Currency:	*lats* and *santīmi*
Area:	40,133 square miles (64,589 square kilometers)
Coastline:	308 miles (497 kilometers) long
Lowest point:	Baltic Sea (0 feet/meters)
Highest point:	Gaizinkalns at 1,024 feet (312 meters)
Longest river:	Gauja River at 280 miles (452 kilometers)

This chart shows maximum temperatures (red), minimum temperatures (blue), and the number of rain days (bars) in Riga throughout the year.

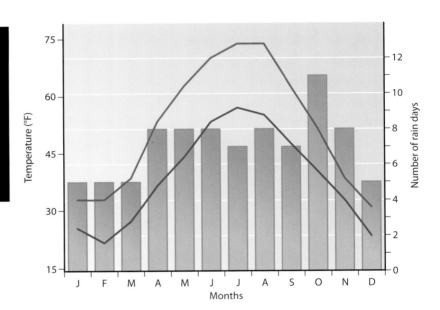

Natural resources:	peat, limestone, **amber**, timber
Main imports:	machinery and heavy equipment, energy, chemicals, some foods
Main exports:	timber, amber, honey, textiles
National symbols:	white wagtail (bird), two-spotted ladybug (insect), daisy (flower)
Famous Latvians:	Mariss Jansons (conductor), Inese Galante (opera singer), Mikhail Baryshnikov (dancer), Uljana Semjonova (basketball player)

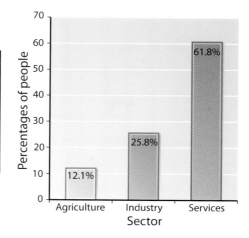

This bar chart shows that in Latvia many more people work in the **service industry** than in other sectors.

Festivals

Latvia has 11 national holidays. They include Midsummer on June 23–24 and **Independence** Day on November 18. Midsummer is also known as Jāni and is one of the Latvians' favorite festivals. It celebrates the longest day of the year. People dress in traditional clothes, build bonfires, and sing folk songs.

Other yearly festivals include the International Baltic Ballet Festival in April, the Baltic Medieval Festival in June, the Jūrmala Pop Festival in July, and Arsenāls film festival in September.

Latvian national anthem

God Bless Latvia was adopted as the national anthem in 1920. It is different from many national anthems because it does not mention war or other national struggles. Instead, it focuses on song and dance. It was written by Kārlis Baumanis in 1873, at a time when **nationalism** was taking hold in Latvia. The first two verses are:

> *God bless Latvia,*
> *Our dearest fatherland,*
> *Do bless Latvia,*
> *Oh, do bless it!*
>
> *Where Latvian daughters bloom,*
> *Where Latvian sons sing,*
> *Let us dance in happiness there,*
> *In our Latvia!*

Timeline

BCE is short for before the Common Era. BCE is added after a date and means that the date occurred before the birth of Jesus Christ, for example, 450 BCE.

CE is short for Common Era. CE is added after a date and means that the date occurred after the birth of Jesus Christ, for example, 720 CE.

around 3000 BCE	Area now known as Latvia is first inhabited
around 2000 BCE	Baltic **tribes** settle along the coast
around 100 CE	**Amber trade** with the Romans flourishes
1200s	Germans invade in an attempt to bring Christianity to Latvia. This group of Germans eventually call themselves the Livonian Brothers of the Sword.
1201	Riga is established as a trading post
1270	The Livonian State is established
1500s	Most of Latvia becomes Lutheran (**Protestant**)
1558–1583	The Livonian War takes place. Poland and Lithuania take over much of present-day Latvia.
1600–1629	The Polish-Swedish War leads to Sweden taking over Riga and the surrounding areas
1600s	Latvian explorers set up colonies in the West Indies
1700–1721	The Great Northern War results in Russia taking over areas of Latvia previously controlled by Sweden, and later the rest of Latvia
1873	The "Latvian Awakening" movement begins
1904	The first Latvian political party , the Latvian Social **Democratic** Workers' Party, is formed

1905	**Revolution** breaks out due to the Latvian people's frustration with Russian rule
1914–1918	World War I takes place. Latvia is divided between Germany and Russia.
1918	Latvia declares its **independence** from Russia
1919–1920	The Liberation war takes place, as Latvians fight for their independence to be recognized
1920	Russia recognizes Latvia's independence
1935	The Freedom Monument is erected in Riga
1939–1945	World War II takes place. Latvia is invaded by the Russians, the Germans, and then the Russians again.
1940	Latvia is made the 15th **republic** of the **Soviet Union**
1988	Political demonstrations for independence take place
1991	Latvia regains independence
1997	Riga Old Town is listed on the **UNESCO World Heritage list**
2001	Riga celebrates its 800th anniversary
2004	Latvia becomes a member of the **EU** and **NATO**
2006	Latvia hosts its first major sporting event, the World Ice Hockey Championships
2006	The NATO summit is held in Riga
2008	Global financial crisis affects Latvia badly, leading to one of the highest unemployment rates in Europe
2009	The Latvian government resigns as a result of the financial crisis

Glossary

amber orange-red stone used in jewelry

citizen person belonging to a country and being part of its society

culture practices, traditions, and beliefs of a society

democracy system of government where the people of a country elect representatives to a parliament

deport make someone leave a country

descendant person who is directly related to another person from a previous generation. A grandchild is a descendant of a grandmother.

dominant most powerful and influential group or person

economy to do with the money, industry, and jobs in a country

elect choose by voting

endangered in danger of extinction

EU (European Union) organization of European countries with shared political and economic aims

exile being forced to leave your country and live somewhere else

export transport and sell goods to another country

head of state main public representative of a country, such as a queen or president

hydroelectric electricity made from the movement of water

import bring in a product, resource, or service from another country

independence having freedom from outside control

migration when animals move from one country to stay in another for a season or longer

minority group of people who differ from most others in their country in their race, religion, culture, or language

national identity sense of belonging to a country and being part of its culture and beliefs

nationalism strong belief in and support of one's own country

NATO (North Atlantic Treaty Organization) organization that includes the United States, Canada, and many European countries in which members give each other military help

pagan religion where many different things are worshipped. Paganism is usually the religion that was practiced before Christianity.

playwright writer of play scripts

pollution when substances make water, air, or soil dirty and harmful to living things

Protestant member of one of the Christian churches that broke away from the Catholic Church in around the 1500s

republic country with an elected leader and no monarch

revolution when large numbers of people try to change the government, using either peaceful or violent protest

rural in the countryside

service industry part of a country's economy that provides services, such as hotels, shops, and schools for its people

Soviet Union communist state made up of Russia and its former empire, in existence between 1922 and 1991

trade buying and selling of goods, usually between countries

tribe independent social group, historically often made up of nomadic peoples

UN (United Nations) organization of many nations started in 1945 to promote world peace and understanding

UNESCO (United Nations Educational, Scientific, and Cultural Organization) agency that helps countries to work together through education, science, and culture

wetland area of marshy, boggy land

World Heritage site place of cultural importance that is protected by a United Nations agency

Find Out More

Books

Aizpuriete, Amanda. *Looking at Latvia*. Minneapolis, MN: Oliver Press, 2006.
Barlas, Robert. *Latvia*. New York: Benchmark Books, 2010.
Docalavich, Heather. *Latvia*. Broomall, PA: Mason Crest Publishers, 2005.

Websites

www.li.lv
This is the official site of the Latvian Institute. It includes information on all aspects of Latvian life.

www.latviatourism.lv/info.php
Find out more about Latvia on this site.

http://news.bbc.co.uk/2/hi/europe/country_profiles/1106666.stm
Scroll down the BBC's country profile on Latvia to learn about some of the country's most important political leaders.

https://www.cia.gov/library/publications/the-world-factbook/geos/lg.html
Visit the Latvia page on the CIA World Factbook website. You can find everything from maps to photographs, as well as a lot of great, up-to-date information for your school projects.

http://www.latvia.travel/en
This website of the Latvian Tourism Development Agency has a lot of good information on Latvia and its great attractions.

Places to visit

If you ever get the chance to go to Latvia, these are some of the places you could visit:

Gauja National Park

There are hiking and cycling trails to follow in this beautiful national park. You could also have a go in a canoe, or visit Turaida Castle for a great view of the Gauja River.

Jūrmala

If you like going to the seaside, Jūrmala is the place for you! This popular resort town has a long coastline of white sandy beaches. You could try a number of activities, such as beach volleyball, tennis, cycling, and water skiing, or toss around a frisbee at the beach.

The Freedom Monument, Riga

The Freedom Monument is one of Latvia's most treasured sites. It celebrates the nation's independence from foreign rule and towers above the buildings around it.

The Occupation Museum, Riga

This museum documents the German and Russian occupations sufffered by the Latvian people during the 1900s. It is said that in order to understand Latvia and the Latvians, travelers should visit this museum.

Kuldiga

Just outside this ancient city, you will find the famous Venta Falls, the widest waterfall in Europe. The Venta River, one of the largest rivers in Latvia, runs through Kuldiga.

Topic Tools

You can use these topic tools for your school projects. Trace the map onto a sheet of paper, using the thick black outlines to guide you.

The Latvian flag was designed in 1917 and has been the official flag since 1990. The red color is known as "Latvian red." Copy the flag design and then color in your picture. Make sure you use the right colors!

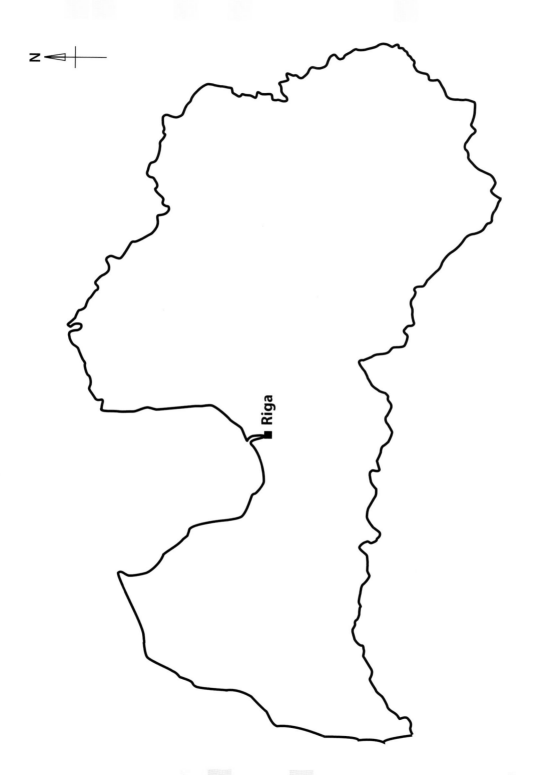

N

Riga

Index

Titles in the series

JUN 1 9 2014
3265